I0414702

Practical Guide to Facing Relaxed Pregnancy, Preparing To Become a Perfect Parent. Right Habit and Healthy Eating. Techniques of Preparation.

DISCLAIMER

The information contained in "Guide on how to have a relaxed pregnancy, Nature Childbirth and Parenting" is meant to serve as a comprehensive collection of strategies that the author of this eBook has done research about. Summaries, strategies, tips and tricks are only recommendations by the author, and reading this eBook will not guarantee that one's results will exactly mirror the author's results.

The author of this eBook has made all reasonable efforts to provide current and accurate information for the readers of this eBook. The author and its associates will not be held liable for any unintentional errors or omissions that may be found. The material in the eBook may include information by third parties. Third party materials comprise of opinions expressed by their owners. As such, the author of this eBook does not assume responsibility or liability for any third party material or opinions.

The publication of third party material does not constitute the author's guarantee of any information, products, services, or opinions contained within third party material. Use of third party material does not guarantee that your results will mirror our results. Publication of such third party material is simply a recommendation and expression of the author's own opinion of that material.

Whether because of the progression of the Internet, or the unforeseen changes in company policy and editorial submission guidelines, what is stated as fact at the time of this writing may become outdated or inapplicable later.

CONTENTS

DESCRIPTION

Every pregnancy is a unique event and different from woman to woman. Many things happen during the 40 weeks of gestation that lead from conception to the birth of the child. Some of these are clearly visible and concern above all the changes of one's body, those of the woman, who accompany the gestation.

Other changes are more "hidden", starting from the growth and development of the fetus. In this book, the result of research on parenting, planning and personal organization, physical and psychological health, right nutrition, you will find indications, practical aid and support, to face your motherhood in a relaxed way, both from a point of view of mental wellbeing and in preparation to become perfect parents in anticipation of childbirth.

Another aspect that is addressed is aimed at the care of the body in respect of its child, providing valuable advice on foods to be introduced and those to avoid in their diet, for a correct nutrition poor in fats, sugars and salt (real enemies undisputed both in the prenatal and breastfeeding periods) with foods rich in vitamins and minerals specific to meet the perfect relationship that binds nutritional needs and the growth of this new life from its first day of conception.

Finally, not all women know that exercise is very useful to prepare for childbirth. Therefore, you will find support to be in shape at the great moment, with relaxation techniques of the mind and physical exercises to reduce the pains and discomfort caused by the weight of the belly, to align the back and enlarge the pelvis to allow the baby to position itself in an optimum way favoring labor.

CHAPTER 1
How To Have A Relaxing Pregnancy

Being pregnant can and should be one of the most exciting and fulfilling times of a woman's life but unfortunately it can also be one of the most stressful times too. Money worries, raging hormones, concerns about the health of the baby and difficulty sleeping, amongst other anxieties, can all turn what should be a special time into a pressure cooker of emotions.

Stress is your body's natural response to events that make you feel threatened or upset. In small doses, it can be helpful making you feel focused and alert. At some point however, it stops being helpful and begins to damage your health, your emotions and your quality of life. Studies have also proved that as early as 17 weeks into a pregnancy stress hormones in the mother are passed into the amniotic fluid; this means that when you are feeling stressed your baby is too.

It's very important therefore to remain as stress-free as possible during pregnancy - eliminating sources of stress, and when this is not possible learning how to cope with it. The first step is learning to recognise the symptoms of stress and this can sometimes be difficult because of the signs mirror some of the normal complaints of pregnancy. Symptoms might include being quick to anger; nail biting; being unable to concentrate; loss of appetite; skin problems; frequent coughs and colds; indigestion; tense muscles; headaches and rapid heartbeat. If you think you are suffering from stress, talk to someone! This could be your partner, family, friends or your midwife. Sometimes just getting it out into the open can be extremely helpful. There are many ways to combat stress which are:

Eat regularly and healthily

Both you and your baby will benefit from healthy nutritious food. During times of stress, it's easy to forget to eat or to reach for the junk food, but the food you eat can have a direct affect on your mood. Stress busting foods include bananas, broccoli, avocados, citrus fruits and whole grain breads, pasta and rice. Try to avoid caffeine too.

Do regular, gentle exercise -this helps to get rid of stress hormones such as adrenaline from your body whilst encouraging the production of endorphins, the "feel good" hormones. Swimming and walking are both ideal during pregnancy. Exercise benefits both your physical and mental health but remember to always consult your doctor before starting an exercise programme.

Try relaxation techniques

Yoga, meditation, and visualization are all good. Practicing every day will help to calm you, and make you less susceptible to stress.

Listen to relaxation music -This is a quick, cheap and effective way to beat stress. Pick something that you enjoy listening to, preferably with a tempo of around 60 bpm. Clinical trials in Taiwan showed that mums who listened to relaxing music during their pregnancies showed a marked decrease in stress, anxiety and depressive symptoms.

Get enough good quality sleep

Try to get into a good bedtime routine - going to bed at roughly the same time each night, having a relaxing bath before bed and making your bedroom as calming as possible. Try to avoid eating too soon before bedtime as this can increase the chances of heartburn.

Take some time out

Call a friend; go for a walk somewhere beautiful; paint your nails; watch a funny film or massage - any of these will help you to put your worries into perspective, and pregnancy is the perfect time to pamper yourself. Nobody can hope to eliminate all the causes of stress in their lives, but by adopting a positive attitude and learning stress management techniques you can have a healthy, happy pregnancy, and if mum is happy then baby is too.

6

CHAPTER 2
Things You Should Know About Your Pregnancy

Pregnancy and childbirth are life altering events for any couple. The birth of a baby is always a special thing to any woman. It brings many new things which you previously did not know. It is strongly encouraged to a pregnant woman to embrace a magical time like this. During this period her own soul allows someone new to enter her own belly.

Understand what is happening

Pregnancy is a phase when you should learn the howling changes that takes place in your body and of an unborn too. You should also learn about the course of childbirth, availability of birthing choices and what to expect in a normal delivery. Also be aware about the expected particular prenatal health status and then develop a birthing plan based on your educated wishes. But please remember that as a birth plan is a list of wishes for your birthing experience, it might differ with changes in your or your baby's, health status. Register and explore the birthing facility before the exact day approaches.

Learn About pain management

Epidurals, though common, involve risks. Low blood pressure, decelerating baby's heart rate, back pain, severe headache, and seizures are all causes of epidural anesthesia. Also the biggest side effect of it is an inability to recognize the natural urge to push your baby out. For this, water birthing is a marvelous birthing option; equally as effective as an epidural. Acupuncture, Reiki, and hypnosis are a few more effective ways of managing pain.

Avoid becoming submissive

It is seen that the expectant parents experience an active role in discouraging submissiveness. In most cases it is seen that the couples are surrendering their experience to the authority of a physician.

Irrespective of considering a highly caring physician that she also has tons of other responsibilities while attending to your birth. Above this many of the procedures suggested are routine and are possibly personalized for your individual birthing experience. For example, you prefer not having intravenous fluids during birth because you desire to walk about unencumbered by an I.V pole.

Yet Intravenous fluids are often routinely ordered, not because the birthing woman is at risk for dehydration, but to ensure easy access for medication administration via I.V route. Your physician may agree to only having intravenous access by the use of a saline-lock.

Consider Expert support

Certified labor support specialists are proven to be a good option for the birthing woman. You can receive emotional support from them and can use some comforting measures like positioning, massage, and effective relaxation techniques during that momentous time.

CHAPTER 3
How To Achieve A Healthy Pregnancy

For most women, pregnancy is a time of great joy, excitement and anticipation. Pregnancy is a time of physical and emotional change when lots of changes occur naturally within your body. If you are a smoker, then use your pregnancy, or the time when you are planning pregnancy to quit smoking and stay quit after the baby is born. Maternal smoking during pregnancy is associated with a higher risk of non-syndromic orofacial clefts in infants. Smoking during pregnancy is a very bad choice. Pregnancy is a time to "listen" to your body - it is not a time to be dieting, and trying to lose weight.

The key to a healthy pregnancy is planning it in the first place. Eating well can help you have a healthy pregnancy and a healthy newborn - Healthy mum, healthy pregnancy. If you try to stay as healthy as you can during your pregnancy this will give you the best chance of delivering a healthy baby at full term.

As an expectant mother, your top priority should be healthy eating. Eating well should begin before you become pregnant so your body will be stocked up with the nutrients you need for a healthy pregnancy. Shortly after finding out that you have conceived you should see a doctor, as your doctor can explain to you about healthy pregnancy weight gain. Staying healthy is doubly important when you're pregnant.

Exercise is also an important part of a healthy pregnancy, exercise can help you return to your pre-pregnancy weight faster and also have a faster, easier birth.

Adequate sleep is essential to promote a healthy pregnancy. Talking with a health care provider is one of the most important things women and families can do to prepare for a healthy pregnancy. Even before conception, it is absolutely essential to plan for a healthy pregnancy.

A healthy lifestyle, even before you become pregnant is the best way to give your baby a healthy start. If you're planning to become pregnant, prepare for a healthy pregnancy by taking care of medical and dental concerns beforehand. Pregnancy is NOT the time to be on a weight loss program.

What Are The
First Symptoms Of Pregnancy?

In my experience, very early symptoms of pregnancy are not always text book. There are many different signs and symptoms of pregnancy, and although most women expect certain symptoms to come with pregnancy, these do vary according to individual women and to their individual pregnancies. The earliest symptoms of pregnancy are generally nausea, fatigue, and breast tenderness, but not everybody experiences these.

Nausea is actually a good sign as it tells the doctor that the pregnancy is likely to be going on well in terms of hormones. The most commonly looked for early sign of pregnancy is missing a menstrual period. Although you may find you have a lot of the symptoms, the only way to truly tell if you are pregnant is to obtain a positive pregnancy test. Blood tests can confirm a pregnancy within days of conception if pregnancy is suspected and you really can't wait to find out. Women should always report worrying signs or symptoms to their doctor during pregnancy.

Pregnancy is an amazing phenomenon of nature that is the core of our existence. One of the easiest and best ways to avoid problems and complications during pregnancy is to get regular medical exams from your doctor or midwife. Pregnancy is an exciting time in a woman's life, and you should take care of yourself and your unborn baby. During pregnancy women are offered a range of tests which are designed to check whether the baby is developing normally and if the pregnancy is going well.

Pregnancy is a very exciting time in most women's lives, but for others an unexpected and unplanned pregnancy is not such welcome news. If the pregnancy is unexpected, you may be feeling scared or confused. This is a usual reaction to an unplanned pregnancy.

There are many organizations that can and will assist, and it is always good to be able to talk to the father, friends and family to help get your feelings into perspective.

5 Steps to
Having a healthy pregnancy

If you've decided to have a baby, the most important thing is that you care a lot, so that both you and the baby are healthy in the future.Girls who receive proper care and make the right decisions are highly likely to have healthy babies.

Prenatal Care

If you discover you are pregnant, see a doctor as soon as possible to begin receiving prenatal care (care during pregnancy). The sooner you begin receiving medical care, the better the chances that both you and your baby are healthy in the future.

If you can not afford to visit a doctor or pay for the consultation in a clinic for prenatal care, social service organizations exist that can help. Ask your parents, school counselor or another trusted adult to help you find resources in your community.

During the first consultation, the doctor will ask a lot of questions, such as date of your last period. In this way, you can calculate how long have you been pregnant and what date to expect your baby.

Doctors estimate the duration of pregnancy in weeks. The due date is estimated, but the majority of babies born between 38 and 42 weeks after the first day of last menstrual period of women, or between 36 and 38 weeks after conception (when the sperm fertilizes the egg). Only a small percentage of women give birth at the estimated delivery date.

The pregnancy is divided into three phases, or quarters. The first quarter runs from conception to end of week 13. The second is from week 14 to 26. The third, from week 27 until the end of pregnancy. The doctor will examine you and perform a pelvic exam.

The doctor will also order blood tests, urine tests and tests to check for sexually transmitted diseases (STD by its acronym in English), including an HIV test, an increasingly common condition in adolescents. (Because some STDs can cause serious health problems in newborns, it is important to get appropriate treatment to protect the baby.)

The doctor will explain what are the physical and emotional changes that you are likely to experience during pregnancy. We also learn to recognize the symptoms of possible problems (complications) during pregnancy. This is essential, because teenagers are at greater risk of experiencing certain complications such as anemia or hypertension, and give birth before the expected date (premature labor).

Your doctor will want you to start taking prenatal vitamins containing folic acid, calcium and iron right away. Your doctor may prescribe vitamins or can recommend a brand you can buy without a prescription. These minerals and vitamins help to ensure the good health of baby and mother, and avoid certain birth defects.

Ideally, you should visit your doctor once a month during the first 28 weeks of pregnancy. Then you should visit every 2 weeks until week 36 and weekly thereafter until delivery. If you have a disease like diabetes, which requires careful monitoring during pregnancy, it is likely that your doctor wants to see you more often.

During consultations, your doctor will monitor your weight, blood pressure and urine, in addition to measuring your belly to go record the baby's growth. When the baby's heartbeat can be heard with a special device, the doctor will listen to every time you visit. It is likely that your doctor will also indicate other tests during pregnancy, such as an ultrasound to make sure the baby is in perfect condition.

Part of prenatal care is to attend classes where women who are expecting a baby learn how to have a healthy pregnancy and delivery, as well as what is the basic care for the newborn. It is likely that these classes are conducted in hospitals, medical centers, schools and universities in your area.

If adults can be difficult to talk to, askyour doctor about your own body. This is even more difficult for adolescents.

12

The role of your doctor is to help you enjoy a healthy pregnancy and have a healthy baby... and it is likely that there is nothing that a pregnant woman has not already asked. So don't be afraid to ask about everything you need to know.

Always be honest when your doctor asking questions, even if they are embarrassing. Many of the issues that your doctor wants you to cover could affect the health of your baby. Think of your doctor as someone who is not only a resource but also a friend you can trust to talk about what is happening to you.

What changes can you expect in your body

Pregnancy creates many physical changes. Here are some of the most common:

Growth of breasts

The increase in breast size is one of the first signs of pregnancy and the breasts may continue to grow throughout pregnancy. It is possible to increase several sizes of support during the course of pregnancy.

Skin changes

Do not be surprised if people comment that your skin looks "glowing" when you're pregnant: pregnancy produces an increased blood volume, which can make your cheeks are a little more pink than usual. In addition, hormonal changes increase the secretion of the sebaceous glands, so that your skin may look brighter. For the same reason, acne is also common during pregnancy

Among other changes that pregnancy hormones generated in the skin are yellowish or brownish spots that appear on the face, which are called melasma, and a dark stripe running from the navel to the pubis, which known as linea nigra. Also, moles or freckles that you had before pregnancy may increase in size or become darker. Even the areola, the area around the nipple becomes darker.

Stretch marks may also occur (thin lines of pink or purple) in the abdomen, breasts or thighs. Except for the darkening of the areola, which is usually permanent, these skin changes will disappear after delivery.

Mood swings

It is very common to experience mood swings during pregnancy. Some girls may suffer from depression during pregnancy or after childbirth. If you have symptoms of depression such as sadness, changes in sleep patterns, desires to hurt yourself or negative feelings about yourself or your life, ask your doctor for advice about starting your treatment.

Pregnancy Discomforts

Pregnancy can cause some unpleasant side effects. Among such disorders, include the following:

•nausea and vomiting, especially during the first months of pregnancy;
•leg swelling;
•varicose veins in the legs and the area around the vaginal opening; hemorrhoids;
•heartburn and constipation;
•back pain;
•fatigue and sleeping problems.

If you suffer from one or more of these side effects, remember that you are not alone. Ask your doctor for advice on how to handle these common problems. If you are pregnant and have bleeding or pain, contact your doctor right away, even if you decided to terminate your pregnancy. What you should avoid

If you smoke, drink alcohol or use drugs during pregnancy, both you and your baby are at risk for serious problems.

Alcohol

At present, doctors believe it is not advisable to drink a drop of alcohol during pregnancy. If you drink alcoholic beverages you can damage the developing fetus and the baby is at risk for birth defects and mental problems.

Smoke

Smoking during pregnancy carries some of the following risks: the birth of a dead fetus (when a baby dies inside the womb), low birth weight (which increases the possibility that the baby has health problems), infants (babies born before 37 weeks) and sudden infant death syndrome (SIDS for its acronym in English). SIDS is the sudden death for no apparent reason of a baby under one year.

Drugs

Illegal drugs such as cocaine or marijuana during pregnancy may cause abortions, premature births and other health problems. In addition, babies can be born with an addiction to certain drugs. If you have trouble quitting smoking, drinking alcohol or using drugs, ask your doctor to help you. Consult your doctor before taking any medication during pregnancy. This includes medicines sold over the counter, prepared herbal supplements and vitamins.

Unsafe Sex

Talk to your doctor about sex during pregnancy. If your doctor allows you to have sex during pregnancy, you should use a condom to avoid contracting a sexually transmitted disease (STD in English). Because some STDs can cause blindness, pneumonia or meningitis in the newborn, it is important for you to protect yourself and protect the baby.

CHAPTER 4
How To Take Care During Pregnancy

Feeding

Many young people are concerned by the appearance of your body and fear of weight gain during pregnancy. But this is not the time to cut calories or go on a diet because you are feeding two people. Both you and your baby need certain nutrients for the baby to grow properly. If you eat a variety of healthy foods, drink enough water and you reduce the junk food, high fat, help both you and the baby to be healthy and growing.

Doctors generally recommend adding about 300 calories a day to the diet, so as to provide the baby with adequate nutrition growth. According to the weight you had before becoming pregnant, you should gain between 11 and 15 kilos (25 to 35 pounds) during pregnancy, mostly during the last 6 months. Your doctor will advise you about this depending on your particular situation.

Eating more fiber, from 25 to 30 grams daily, and drinking enough water can help prevent common problems such as constipation. Fruits and vegetables and whole grain breads, cereals or whole wheat muffins are good sources of fiber.

It is necessary that you avoid some foods and beverages during pregnancy, such as:

•some types of fish such as swordfish, canned tuna and other fish that may have a high content of mercury (your doctor can help you decide which fish to eat);
•foods containing raw eggs, such as mousse or salad type "Caesar";
•raw meat, fish or undercooked;
•processed meats such as sausages or cold cuts;
•Unpasteurized soft cheeses such as feta, brie, blue or goat, and milk, unpasteurized juice or cider.

It is also desirable to limit the consumption of artificial sweeteners and caffeine and artificial sweeteners.

If you want to pursue healthy nutrition during your pregnancy, it is important to choose the right foods to eat when pregnant. Good nutrition is closely linked to prevention of a number of pregnancy problems such as placental abruption, preeclampsia, anaemia and pre-mature birth. Expectant women should eat a combination of pregnancy foods from the different food groups. However, your pregnancy calls for some unique dietary requirements. Understanding the proper combination of foods to eat when pregnant is one of the main secrets to a healthy pregnancy.

When you have a baby growing inside you, consuming enough proteins is important. Proteins are important for the development of major organs. Proteins help in the formation of red blood cells, which as you know are very important as you are producing extra blood for the proper development of the growing fetus. Pregnant women who consume at least 80 grams of protein a day are reported to lessen the likelihood of developing pregnancy problems like toxaemia and eclampsia. As expected, the best way to increase protein consumption is to choose pregnancy foods rich in protein.

These include chicken and beef, dairy products such as cheese, yogurt and milk, along with nuts, beans and eggs. Taking in enough nutrients from carbohydrates is also crucial during pregnancy. Nourishing both you and your baby takes up a lot of energy. It is carbohydrates that allow us to feel energized. Some of the carbohydrate-rich foods to eat when pregnant include rice, breads, vegetables, fruits, pasta, cereals and potatoes. These foods are also rich in fiber, making them even more desirable as healthy pregnancy foods. Foods rich in calcium (dairy foods) such as milk, yogurt and cheese are a must for proper pregnancy nutrition.

To ensure your baby's proper bone development, you need to take in at least 900 to 1200mg of calcium. Furthermore, iron-rich foods are also important. Your body needs more iron than usual in order to support the extra blood supply required.

Foods rich in vitamin C, vitamin A and folic acid, are also good pregnancy foods that can do wonders to you and your baby's health.

Pregnant women must also take vitamin and mineral supplements. Although wise choices on what food to eat when pregnant can be enough for a healthy pregnancy, dietary supplements help make sure that you are indeed getting all the nutrients needed for proper development. Lastly, it is important for pregnant mothers to make sure they are hydrated enough.

Drink lots of fruit juices, soups, vegetable juices, filtered water and sugar-free soft drinks. Understanding the correct foods to eat when pregnant can help you manage your pregnancy correctly. Although morning sickness in the first trimester may make things difficult for you, making sure that you eat right is one less thing to worry about. Exercise

Exercising during pregnancy is good for your health when you have no complications with the pregnancy and choose appropriate activities. Doctors generally recommend low-impact activities such as walking, swimming and yoga. In general, you should avoid contact sports and high impact aerobic activities that pose a higher risk of injury. It is also not recommended to do a job that involves heavy lifting for women during pregnancy. Talk to your doctor if you have questions about what kind of exercises are safe for you and your baby.

Sleep

It is important to get plenty of rest during pregnancy. During the first months of pregnancy, trying to acquire the habit of sleeping on your side. As pregnancy progresses, lying on your side, knees bent, will be the most comfortable position. It will facilitate the functioning of the heart, since the baby's weight will not exert any pressure on the vein that carries blood from the feet and legs back to the heart.

Some doctors specifically recommend that pregnant girls should sleep on their left side. Because some of the major blood vessels are in the right side of the abdomen, lying on the left side helps keep the uterus from putting pressure on them. Ask your doctor what your recommendation. In most cases, the trick is to lie on either side, to reduce pressure on the back.

Throughout the pregnancy, but particularly in the later stages, it is likely that you wake up frequently at night to go to the bathroom. While it is important to drink plenty of water during pregnancy, try to drink more during the day instead of night. Go to the bathroom before bed. As the pregnancy progresses, you might be hard to find a comfortable position in bed. You can try placing pillows around and under the stomach, back or legs to feel more comfortable.

Stress can also affect sleep. Perhaps you're concerned about the health of the baby, birth, or how it will play this new role of mother. All these feelings are normal but can produce insomnia. Talk to your doctor if you have trouble sleeping during pregnancy.

Emotional Health

It is common for pregnant adolescents experience a variety of emotions such as fear, anger, guilt, confusion and sadness. Maybe you take some time to adjust to the fact that you are having a baby. It means a huge change and it is natural for pregnant teens wonder if they are ready for the responsibilities involved in becoming mothers.

The feelings of a young often depend on how much support received by the baby's father, his family (and family of the baby's father) and his friends.

The situation of each youth is different. Depending on your situation, you may need to seek more support for people who are not part of your family. It is important to talk with people who can support you, guide you and help you share and sort out your feelings.

In some cases, teenage pregnancies and spontaneous abortions have lost the baby. This can be very sad and difficult to overcome for some, but to others it causes a feeling of relief. It is important to talk about these feelings and receive support from friends and Family.

CHAPTER 5
What You Should Know About Pregnancy Massage And How It Helps To Have A Relaxed Pregnancy

Pregnancy massage or prenatal massage are generic terms used to describe a variety of conditions and treatments performed to help alleviate the signs and symptoms associated with pregnancy.

Conditions like: Sciatica, headaches, low back pain, swelling in the extremities, muscle tension and sleep disturbances can all be part of being pregnant. An RMT can work to address all these conditions.
What are the benefits of a pregnancy massage?

There are so many benefits to having a pregnancy massage. At no time in your life will you undergo so much change in your body over such a short period of time. Aches, pains and body changes can be greatly decreased when you consult an RMT.

An RMT is an individual who is registered with the College of Massage Therapists in accordance with the Regulated Health Professions Act and the Massage Therapy Act. ... A Registered Massage Therapist is a primary healthcare provider and anyone may visit an RMT of their choice.

Treatments that respond well to pregnancy massage are: Sciatica, headaches, muscle tension, swelling in the extremities and low back pain.Clients report better sleep patterns and over all feeling of being relaxed and more connected to their body.When receiving a pregnancy massage, how should I be positioned?

Positioning is the most important part of a treatment. You want to take in account how far along the pregnancy is, the further along it is the more you will need to look at supporting the body. In general, sideline is best. This is because it allows the most amount of modification to the body position.

Resting on your stomach puts too much pressure on your abdomen and breasts. There are pregnancy tables that have a hole cut where the abdomen is and this is replaced with a stretchy fabric that makes a hammock for your growing belly to rest on.

There is some controversy about these tables because depending on the tension on the hammock it can lead to not enough support for your belly. This can put undue stress on your abdominal and pelvic ligaments.

This can be very serious depending on how far you are along and if it has been a difficult pregnancy or not. I highly suggest consulting with your massage therapist to discuss this issue. Resting on your back can position your uterus to put pressure on the returning veins from the lower extremity. This again needs to be discussed as your pregnancy progresses.

Precautions for pregnancy massage
.

Make sure the RMT(Registered Massage Therapist) does a thorough history and assessment before the treatment begins. Clients tend to want to rush to the treatment and they sometime over look very serious contraindications for treatment. Please make sure to discuss everything about your pregnancy with your RMT.Some precautions for pregnancy massages are diabetes, miscarriages and varicosities in the lower extremity.

CHAPTER 6
Stress And Pregnancy – Learning To Reduce Stress For Pregnancy Relaxing

For most women pregnancy is a special time. It is also a time of considerable change, therefore stress and pregnancy is quite common as a woman struggles to come to terms with these changes. This content is all about stress and pregnancy, what causes it and some simple tips to help you reduce it and have a stress free pregnancy. Most of us experience varying levels of stress on a daily basis, when a woman is faced with coping with everyday stress and pregnancy.

In addition, she also has to come to terms with changes in her body and her emotions, together with how her pregnancy will affect her family, financial and work situation.

Managing stress during pregnancy

For many it can be difficult to adequately manage stress and pregnancy while remaining in control of situations that until now have been easy to cope with. Although stress and pregnancy can add additional worry, stress does not have to be all bad and we all need a little bit of stress in order to perform well.Learning to manage stress effectively provides us with the drive we need to meet new challenges.

For a pregnant woman coping with stress and pregnancy means understanding and embracing the changes, being prepared, taking good care of herself (inside and out), feeling energised rather than drained, not being afraid to ask for help and making the necessary adjustments, in order to continue functioning well at home and at work. When stress and pregnancy do become a worry then physical or emotional stress builds up to uncomfortable levels and this can be dangerous.

In the short term, this can cause anxiety, headache, backache, fatigue, sleeplessness, or poor appetite. Long term stress and pregnancy can contribute to high blood pressure, heart disease, lowered resistance to infectious disease, and risk to the fetus.

22

What can you expect?

Most pregnant women will experience nausea, frequent urination, swelling, backache and fatigue. Hormonal changes may contribute to mood swings and there will be some anxiety about the health of her unborn child, her ability to cope with labor and birth, and her ability to be a good mother. ...And how can you cope?

The good news is that for most women stress is unlikely to cause problems in pregnancy. A pregnant woman can cope with stress and pregnancy by:

•Recognizing that the symptoms are temporary
•Identify the personal and work-related sources of stress
•Eat a healthy diet and not skip meals
•Get plenty of sleep
•Avoid alcohol, cigarettes and drugs
•Do gentle regular exercise (with your doctors consent)
•Form a good support network
•Set aside some time every day to practise relaxation

Diet & Stress

It is necessary to understand the importance of a healthy diet, regular meals, the benefits of regular relaxation, and the other points mentioned in order to better cope with stress and pregnancy. A good diet is essential not just for you, but also for the nutrition of your unborn baby.

Sources of stress relief

Many childbirth educators offer childbirth preparation classes that can help reduce stress during pregnancy and can advise on relaxation and staying healthy during pregnancy. A good relaxation CD will not only prove useful to alleviate stress during pregnancy and make you feel better, but can also be very beneficial in preparing you to relax your mind and your muscles during labour and birth.Women who are still concerned about coping with stress and pregnancy should talk with their GP (a doctor based in the community who treats patients with minor illness and refers those with serious conditions to a hospital) or healthcare provider..

CHAPTER 7
Using Pregnancy Meditations To Relax And Empower You

Pregnancy and giving birth can be an exhilarating, empowering and happy experience. Yet, so often this beautiful, natural process evolves into a hard, distressing, sometimes complicated procedure. Women's bodies have been well designed to give birth, yet we can sabotage our own pregnancy and labour by holding onto negative beliefs and fears.

These negative beliefs and fears, if not recognised, released and dealt with, will lock up and constrict important muscles and organs in our body preventing them from doing what they do best. Negative beliefs & fears are the major factors of difficult pregnancies and labours.
We are bombarded with stories and myths about pregnancy and birth. They have been passed down and around, from generation to generation, from girlfriend to girlfriend, husbands to husbands. They can be alive and as fearful as ever, resonating deep within our minds and bodies.

I don't know how many times I've heard the analogy of "having a baby" to being the equivalent of passing a watermelon through the bowels of our being, and that's putting it politely. Well it resonated well within my mind. It was a frightening picture; a frightful thought I carried through my pubescent years and into adulthood.

After the birth of my first baby, I couldn't wait to get home from hospital and tell anyone who wanted to listen. "Yes, It felt just like I was told!" A watermelon, only bigger and far worse! How gutsy and lucky I was to survive such an experience I bragged. The pain, gore and the drugs I described in fine detail until everyone was squirming. "And where was my husband when I needed him?"

24

He was eating the breakfast I'd ordered for myself, in another room! Oh yes, I was the heroine of all heroines, who successfully produced a baby under very difficult circumstances!

Yes, we all squirm and giggle when we hear such stories, but it is because of these stories and myths we do have fears and negative thoughts lurking in our subconscious. We also have our own life to deal with - our relationships, our finances and work commitments. Quite often we shove any concerns about our life down and away when, we don't want to deal with them. But remember they tense, tighten and constrict our bodies. The best environment for a fetus to nourish and grow is a relaxed, stress free body, where blood and oxygen flows freely into important organs and muscles.

So how can you deal with this fear factor?

Most people are so good at putting things away they don't want to know about, talk about, or feel. They don't give themselves a chance to stop and look at these issues. Instead, they busy their lives up even more, so they don't have to 'GO THERE'.

Meditation is an important self-help techni□ue in aiding you to gently sit and relax into a state of peace and calm where you can eventually acknowledge and release fears and negative thoughts in a healthy positive way.

Meditation takes your attention from the outside world, and brings your focus into yourself, just by closing your eyes and following your breath in and out takes your mind off the things you should be doing, the things you've got to do, and the things you should have said and done. Yes, you finally slow down your fast mind, and busy body, by simply focusing on your breath.

Imagery, visualisation is a very effective form of releasing your fears and concerns from a deep cellular level. In a relaxed meditative state, you can visualize passing your fears and concerns over to a higher guidance, a spiritual being or a loved one who has passed from this life where they will take it to a place of healing. This will bring a sense of relief, and deeper relaxation.

As a pregnant woman, having relaxed with your breath, released your fears and in a state of deeper relaxation you can then visualize travelling into your body to your baby. You can explore your uterus, and your birth canal. You can feel and listen to your own body and your own needs. You can feel and listen to your baby's needs. Each time, you will gather more faith and trust in yourself and your own abilities.

As a labouring mum to be, you can use your breath for focus and relaxation. You can breathe into your body as it contracts, not fearing the pressure/pain but using it. You can travel into your body to encourage and reassure yourself and your baby of your inner-strengths. You can visualize your uterus relaxing and filling with energy, your womb, softening and opening for your baby's entry into the world.

Yes, pregnancy and giving birth can be an exhilarating, empowering and happy experience. Know your baby's emotions are dependent on yours; being calm, happy and positive makes for a calm, happy and positive baby trusting in their own abilities.

CHAPTER 8
Pregnancy Care – An Important Step For A Smooth Pregnancy

Pregnancy care is an all important aspect for a pregnant woman. It is significant in terms of its advantages for expectant mothers. While being pregnant makes you feel special, some simple but critical precautions also become mandatory. If followed, these simple steps can make your special moment even more special. Apart from regular medical check-ups, few simple cautionary steps can also make all the difference. They not only make your pregnancy easier but also safer.

Some Crucial Things to Do

Here are some uncomplicated ways to make your child bearing period a special moment in your life. These things are important to keep in mind while you are pregnant.

Have a Balanced Diet

Having a balanced diet is definitely a significant and positive pregnancy care step. As a pregnant woman, always try and have a highly nutritious diet. It should contain all essential nutrients including vitamins, carbohydrates, minerals, and proteins in right proportions. Never binge on uncooked or semi cooked food products especially eggs, meat and fish. Some fish contain high mercury levels and may harm your baby.

Same may be said about semi cooked eggs and meat. Always eat fresh vegetables, fruits and other dairy products. Remember consuming un-pasteurized milk or related products may also be equally dangerous. Do not consume too much of caffeine either. Instead, restrict your caffeine consumption to a maximum of 2 cups per day.
Avoid working too much

During pregnant stage, it becomes absolutely essential that complete prenatal care is in place. One way to ensure that is abandon work till the time you deliver baby. If you are a working lady, apply for maternity leaves well in advance. During final stages of pregnancy, any type of work may lead to unnecessary pressure on womb. This may further disturb healthy growth of the fetus.

Do not lift heavy objects and remain away from heavily reactive metals such as mercury, copper and lead. Do not ever expose yourself to harmful sunrays like ultraviolet radiations as they may harm the baby.

Supplement to Take

Although as discussed above, a natural diet remains the best eating option during pregnancy period, some food supplements may also prove quite healthy. For example, folic acid, a major food supplement is necessary for a good development of your fetus. It helps prevent conditions including spina bifida. However, intake of folic acid should start before becoming pregnant. Other supplements including pain killers, vitamins and other over-the-counter medicines must be taken under direct supervision of your physician. If proper heed is not paid, they can cause birth defects and other serious medical conditions.

Exercise Regularly

By exercising regularly, several pregnancy-related problems may be dealt with easily. It can come in really handy, since it can make childbirth and labor immensely easily. Some recommended exercises include swimming and walking. However, in the event of any discomfort during exercise, do not hesitate to call your doctor. Some symptoms of discomfort while exercising are dizziness, abdomen or chest pain and blurred vision. Under all these circumstances consulting a medical practitioner for advice is good enough.

CHAPTER 9
Things Not To Do During Pregnancy

Apart from things to do, you should be aware of things not to do. These are general precautionary measures to be followed by an expectant mother. Some of them are given below

No Smoking

It includes both active and passive smoking.

No alcohol

Consumption during pregnancy might lead to adverse effects such as fetal alcohol syndrome or birth defects.

Avoiding General Discomfort

Some discomfort during pregnancy is normal. You feel morning sickness and tiredness. Frequent urination, constipation and varicose veins are other such conditions of discomfort. In order to avoid these discomforts, take in lots of water, eat fiber rich food, consume green leafy vegetables and have small meals after frequent intervals.

Pregnancy care without any doubt is a critical and important step towards a safe and relaxed pregnancy. Be careful and follow a healthy life style. At the same time take your doctor's advice to deal with any untoward incident.

Preparing For
The Birth Of A Child

It is also important for you to ensure that the house is maintained properly and that any work that needs to be done on the home before the baby arrives is taken care of in advance.
If the child is the first child, it is likely that you are unaware of how much time is going to be spent on taking care of the child at first. you may think that you have all the time in the world to get things ready around the home, and you may even envision that you are going to be able to work on the home once the child arrives.

This can result in a lot of frustration for you as the dreams are going to quickly give way to reality and the fact that having a young child in the home is quite a lot of work. It is a good idea for you to prepare the home in advance so that you can move into the home stress-free with the new child.

Something else that needs to be considered is that the safety of the child is going to be looked after carefully when it comes to working on the home. Not only are you going to need to make sure that the room itself is safe, such as putting plugs into receptacles and making sure that no window blind cords are going to cause a hazard.

You also want to consider the fact that the paint fumes from the painting of the room are also going to be a hazard for the child. Most parents wait until the last minute to paint the room, and it may look fresh and new but that smell is going to be hard on the child's delicate lungs. Make sure you paint a room far enough in advance so those fumes can be kept to a minimum.

Finally, don't think that you are going to be fine with a few baby bath towels and a box of diapers. Make sure that you load up with plenty of these items, as you are able to do so, and perhaps suggest to others that they load them up as well.

CHAPTER 10
5 Essentials For Preparing For Your First Child

Becoming a parent is a wonderful and yet incredibly scary time of your life. In order to make the transition from couple to family, it is important to make some preparations to ease that transition. Here are some essential preparations that you should make before your child arrives. Take a class in Childbirth or Parenting Generations ago, most children were born at home.

Families were large and most older children helped their parents to take care of the younger siblings in the family. The reality was that most people had an inkling of what to expect when they became parents. Most women also had an idea of what to expect during childbirth. Today, some parents have never held a baby or seen a baby before they have their own child. If you have limited experience, you may consider taking some classes to learn what to expect.

Take A Look At Your Finances

If you are thinking about having a baby, you should be thinking about your finances. For example, you might want to take steps to reduce your credit card debt. You may also want to set aside money for emergencies or to help you pay your bills if you are taking some time off after the birth of your child.

Find A Pediatrician For Your Child

Before your child is born, you will need to find him or her a doctor. Depending upon your insurance plan, you may have a limited amount of options, or you may have quite a few choices. Take the time to review your choices and to find out information on each doctor. Then, choose the doctor that will fit best with your family. For example, if you want to use herbal remedies as well as traditional medicine, you will need to find a doctor that is comfortable with that philosophy. Choosing a doctor who strictly uses traditional medicine can cause a lot of stress on you and your doctor in the future.

Purchase the Essentials

Although your family might be holding a baby shower for you before the birth of your baby, you should probably still plan on purchasing some of the items by yourself. Things you will definitely need are a crib, a car seat, clothes, bottles or breastfeeding equipment, and diapers!

Decide on A Feeding Plan

You should decide how you want to feed your baby before it is born. You may decide to breastfeed your baby, or you may decide to bottle feed your baby. If you are breastfeeding, you might wish to read up on the subject before your baby arrives or take a class in breastfeeding. If you are bottle feeding, you will want to choose a bottle type.

Of course, preparing for the arrival of a baby can take some time. It has often been said that this is why pregnancy lasts for nine months! Take some time to prepare for the birth of your baby now and you will be glad that you did so when your little one arrives.

CHAPTER 11
How To Reduce The Risks Of A Child Birth Defect

To date, even doctors cannot tell us how how and why exactly a child birth defect occurs. Given this, many couple planning pregnancy cannot help but worry. - What can we do to help lessen the risks of having to deal with child birth defect? How do we make sure that our baby comes out healthy? The percentage of child birth defect risk is only 4% vis-a-vis the 96% of healthy newborns.

Nevertheless, expecting parents still want to get as much birth defects information as they can in order to help lessen the risks of having a baby with a defect. Before you plan to get pregnant, observing a few steps will help you reduce the risks not only of a difficult pregnancy but also of giving birth to a baby with a birth defect.

The first trimester of pregnancy is very crucial. It plays a very important role in the development of a child. Given this, good health for the mother is very essential in order to ensure a healthy and safe pregnancy. The sad part is that, most women do not realize that they are pregnant until a few weeks after the conception. One important step to take to help you prepare for your pregnancy is by doing a pre-pregnancy examination.

This process is also called preconception care and is performed by your doctor before you even get pregnant. During your preconception check-up, your physician will assess your overall health and identify risk factors which can complicate your pregnancy. This allows women to prepare in advance in order to ensure they are at their healthiest condition by the time that they get pregnant. Below are some of the benefits which pregnant women can get from a preconception

Examination

Assessment of the family medical history -The doctor can assess your paternal and maternal medical history. This will help determine if you have any family members who have medical conditions like mental retardation, blood pressure and diabetes.

Genetic testing

All possible genetic disorders which can be inherited by the baby may be assessed during the preconception examination. Some of the common genetic birth defects include sickle cell anemia which is a serious blood disorder and the Tay-Sachs disease which is a breakdown disorder which comes with physical and progressive mental retardation. These genetic disorders can be detected through blood exams before the pregnancy.

Personal medical history

Your personal medical history will help determine health conditions which can require special care during your pregnancy. Some of these deficiencies include anemia, high blood pressure, epilepsy and allergies. Your previous surgeries will also be taken into consideration. Your past pregnancies will also be studied especially complications (if any), the number and the length of pregnancy and the number of pregnancy losses.

Vaccination

Your current vaccinations will be assessed to ensure immunity to German measles or rubella. As we all know contracting such disease during pregnancy can be very risky for the baby and can even cause birth defects and miscarriage.

Yes, nobody can tell if your baby will have a child birth defect but every parent can help reduce the risks of having to deal with one by taking the necessary precautions such as by doing the preconception examination.

CHAPTER 12
Exercise And Child Birth Methods

Questions were raised from Pregnant Mothers about how safe they are while participating in exercise since some are restricted while some are allowed. There are proper guidelines needed to protect the mothers and the baby from adverse reactions. Pregnant mothers should be concerned that exercise is necessary to build strong muscles, assisting weight gain, or boost your heart rate in preparation for a tedious labor and delivery.

Also, the importance of exercise is to prevent circulatory stasis in the lower extremities. To love the idea, well planned exercise must be chosen in her line of interest. A recent study showed that pregnant women participating in aerobic exercise have reduced risk of cesarean birth. Those who had regular activity during the first two trimesters of pregnancy have normal birth delivery.

The recommended exercise program consist of:

•5 minutes of warm up exercise
•Stimulus phase of 20 minutes
•5 minutes of cool down exercises
Planned exercise programs have long term benefits such as:
•Weight control
•Decrease incidence of ovarian cancer
•Lower cholesterol Level
•Reduce risk of osteoporosis
•Increase energy level
•Maintain healthy body weight
•Decrease risk of heart disease
•Increase self esteem
•Possible reduction in the chance of cesarean birth

Walking and swimming is the best activity since it promotes exercise to large muscle groups rhythmically. The restricted activities during pregnancy are skiing, cycling, jogging, high impact aerobics program, and long distance swimming. The use of hot tubs and saunas after workouts must not be longer than 5 minutes.

Discontinue exercise immediately if there bleeding occurs. Remember to consult your Physician or midwife before doing any exercise. Exercise promotes a healthy pregnancy leading to a successful, less complicated delivery of the baby.

CHAPTER 13
The Process Of Natural Childbirth

Natural childbirth is defined as a birth that attempts to minimize the intervention of modern medicine, including the use of medications and/or surgical procedures. Experts who believe that natural childbirth is beneficial to both the mother and child feel that anaesthetics may increase the possibility of complications during birth due to the fact that the woman may not be capable of pushing properly during the final stages of delivery.

Natural childbirth often promotes a healthier delivery overall because it eliminates the risks associated with caesarean sections and possible side effects from certain medications. Lamaze is a technique that is designed to help women who choose to deliver via natural childbirth and provides direction in breathing and relaxation. Regular classes are given at local hospitals or clinics by a qualified individual. The father of the child is usually present for each class in order to provide support for the mother. In most cases, the father of the child will also be in the delivery room, which is why it is so important that he also be present to help learn how to coach the mother on breathing and relaxation exercises.

Not all physicians believe that natural childbirth is a positive experience, noting the pain involved as being difficult for the mother. Others believe that it is beneficial as the process of natural childbirth leaves the new mother feeling empowered and also allows her to be alert as the child is brought into the world and placed in her arms.

Depending on the expectant mother's overall health, certain medical intervention may often be required in order to ensure a successful and safe childbirth. Whether or not a natural childbirth is an option will be assessed by the physician and the expectant mother.

Unless it is a matter of life and death or extreme concern as to the health of the mother or child, the choice will ultimately be left up to the mother as she will have the final say in the delivery method. It is advisable, however, that women listen to their physician and carefully consider his/her recommendations.

This content is to be used for informational purposes only and is not intended to be used as professional medical advice. The information contained herein should not be used in place of, or in conjunction with, a doctor's recommendation. Prior to deciding either for or against natural childbirth, the expectant mother must consult a licensed physician for proper diagnosis and a recommendation.

9 Natural Childbirth Myths

When weighing your options for childbirth, it helps if you have accurate information about the options available to you. Unfortunately childbirth is an area where myth often pervades fact. What you hear may have started as truth, but has become such a distorted version, there isn't much truth left. Here are ten of the most common misunderstandings about natural childbirth and the truth behind them.

You have to have a super-high pain tolerance.

Hardly anybody likes pain, and it is easy to assume giving birth causes large amounts of pain so only the most pain tolerant women can do it. What is less well known is how a woman's body increases endorphin levels during labor. This means as the intensity of the contractions build, so does her ability to handle them. Also, contractions peak at about 30 seconds. This means once your contractions become about a minute long they may increase in duration (get longer), but they do not tend to continue building in intensity.

It feels like pulling your lower lip over your head.

I enjoy a good comedy routine, but we shouldn't base our understanding of childbirth on stand up comedy. After having given birth without medication twice, I can most assuredly promise you it feels nothing like pulling on your lips. The parts of the body needed for childbirth are designed to stretch and make room for baby - your lower lip is not designed to be pulled over your head.

You have to be at home to do it.

Homebirth is an option, but it is only one option. Women interested in natural childbirth can also give birth in birth centers or hospitals. It is not the location that matters, but the support you have to help you through contractions. While hospitals have access to medications and emergency equipment, many also have birth tubs, balls and flexible staff who will work with a family to achieve the birth they desire. Hiring a doula gives you even more support and increases your chances of giving birth naturally.

Women become screaming lunatics, yelling at their husbands.

Childbirth is not a psychosis where a woman suddenly takes on a new personality. Although in the earlier half of the 20th century women were given labor drugs that made them act very strange indeed, becoming crazy isn't a part of the natural childbirth process. What does happen is a woman uses all her energy to focus on the work she is doing and distraction makes this harder. Women in hard labor will use the least amount of energy to communicate - this may mean body language, grunts or one word commands. Without the understanding that this behavior is normal, a support person can feel as if they have somehow upset the laboring mother.

Childbirth is the worst pain you will ever feel.

A childbirth educator's husband figured out from her normal 12 hour labor that the time she spent in pain in contractions totaled to about 3 and a half hours.

You can be in pain longer than that for a migraine. And unlike other types of pain, contractions build to a peak, release from the peak and then give you a break. Even in a longer than average labor, there are breaks between contractions. In a 12 hour labor, you might not even need to work through contractions until the last 2 or 3 hours before pushing because most of the time you spend in labor is early labor.

If they know you want a natural childbirth, the nurses won't give you anything for the pain.

Wanting a natural childbirth and achieving a natural childbirth are two different things. While most doulas, nurses and midwives will work with you to achieve your goal of a natural childbirth, they never force you to give birth without medication. Whether or not to use medical pain relief remains your choice regardless of what type of labor you prepared for.

There is no reason to go through labor pain anymore.

There have been ointments and herbs to treat labor pain as far back as the Roman Empire, and probably further back than that. There are also positions and non-medical techniques that work extremely well for keeping mothers comfortable and helping labor progress. It isn't so much the use of a treatment to manage pain that bothers modern women as much as it is the possible side effects and risks of using the treatments.

There is a big difference between the risks of having a massage in labor and having an epidural. Although the massage may not eliminate all the pain, if it allows the woman to labor without having to add the risks of an epidural then why not use it? Studies show just the change of using a doula for additional support decreases requests for pain medication while also decreasing needs for additional medical interventions.

It should more rightly be said that with all we know today, there is no reason to add the risks of medical pain relief to manage labor pain anymore.

40

Women used to die giving birth. Yes, and women still die giving birth.

It has nothing to do with the natural childbirth process. Instead, factors such as poor nutrition, infection and inadequate sanitation are the causes of high mortality rates. In fact, the highest childbirth mortality rate happened because birth was moved to the hospital and infection spread quickly among laboring women when doctors didn't wash their hands. Pain medications increase the risks of having a problem in labor, not reduce them. Cesarean birth adds the increased risks of surgery to childbirth, which means for a normal, healthy pregnancy your risk of dying from childbirth goes up.

I don't need to prepare to give birth, it's a natural process.
While your body is doing the work with or without you, how you respond to labor will have a large impact on how well labor progresses and the amount of pain or discomfort you feel. Knowing positions, tricks and techniques for labor greatly improves your chances of being successful at giving birth naturally, and greatly improves your chances of staying comfortable during labor.

It takes physical and mental energy to labor; if you haven't practiced natural childbirth techniques enough to use them without thinking you won't be able to use them during labor. Preparing for a natural childbirth doesn't necessarily guarantee you will give birth without medications, but not preparing almost always guarantees you will use medications.

CHAPTER 14
Why Do People Choose Natural Childbirth?

With all the painkillers available in this present age to help women tackle the pain of childbirth, there are some who still opt for natural childbirth and this baffles many of those who do not understand why they made this choice. After all, since modern medicine has become so advanced and can help tackle the pain of childbirth, why not just make use of this pain relief option during childbirth?

Long before painkillers were invented, women have always given birth naturally. In fact, most of these women had more than one child. Thus we need to understand that our female body has always been and always will be designed for childbearing and delivery. All that is needed from us woman is to trust in our bodies and not underestimate our capability to endure the pain of childbirth.

Talking about natural childbirth, is all that pain worth it? Of course, it isn't! Unless you understand the need for it. Studies have shown that non-medicated childbirth proceeds faster than medicated childbirth. This is because with each contraction, a signal is sent to your brain to release more hormones that further stimulate this birth process. However if anesthesia was used and the senses dulled, then this signal relay gets impeded and the process of childbirth slows. With this slowdown, pain persists for longer.

More drugs would be needed to help childbirth proceed 'normally' again or maybe eventually a Cesarean section might be called for. It is also important to know that there is no safe anesthesia - be it for the mother or the baby. If nutrients can pass from the mother to the baby via the placenta, can we be sure that the anesthesia will not?

But what if the pain gets intolerable? If there's a will, there's a way! And indeed there are many ways available to help women decrease the pain of childbirth without any medication. However, the premise for most of this methods is that no anesthesia had been used previously.

This is because following the usage of such drugs, the woman's movements become restricted and her senses too dulled to enable proper participation in her labour. Without anything to distract her mind from the pain coupled with the loss of control over her labor, the woman starts to feel insecure. Insecurity breeds tension and fear, which results in more pain as her muscles tense up and her mind starts disbelieving that she can carry out childbirth without the use of anesthesia.

In this present age, not many women will choose to give birth naturally. However if they are able to cast aside their insecurities and learn to manage their fear, natural childbirth might actually be a better choice.

Unassisted Natural Childbirth
Or Medical Childbirth - Which is Better?

The debate between unassisted natural childbirth and medical childbirth continues to rage. The medical profession argues that giving birth in a hospital is safer in case a medical problem arises during the process, while those who support freebirthing declare that most problems occur due to medical intervention. So who is right and who is wrong? The answer is neither. It should be up to the mom-to-be what method she chooses to bring her baby into the world.

There are those who believe that any chemical pain relief or surgical intervention may harm both mom and baby. Others simply want to be in control of their own body during the birth process. Some moms are perfectly happy to hand the whole process over to their pediatrician and that's perfectly OK. Everyone has to do what they feel is right and not be bullied into a course of action which they may regret later.

So what is an unassisted natural childbirth? Can a mom who has for instance an epidural or pain killing drugs claim to have given birth naturally? Does it actually matter? The important thing is to bring your baby into the world safely and without suffering more discomfort than you can tolerate. Some women have an easy birth, others have a high tolerance for pain while still others find the whole birth process frightening.

The important thing is not to feel guilty if you have your heart set on giving birth the natural way and you find you need pain relief during the process.

The important thing is to bring baby into the world safely while still maintaining your own well being so that you can look after your baby when you get home.

If you have chosen an unassisted birth, you may want to take some childbirth classes to help you cope with labor especially if you are not planning on using pain relief such as an epidural. Opt for classes held outside of the hospital system as many hospitals do not support natural childbirth. Classes that teach the Bradley Method or Hypnobirthing are very popular. If you have a supportive partner, get them involved in the process. If you are going solo, consider hiring a doula who can help support you both physically and emotionally throughout the birth process.

Birthing centers are ideal for moms who are healthy and confident they will not require medical attention. These centers encourage unassisted natural childbirth, however it is important not to put your health, or your child's health at risk, because you are determined to give birth naturally. If you have any doubts about your ability to cope, there is no shame in having a medical childbirth. It's up to you!

Different Approaches
To Natural Childbirth

The definition of natural childbirth is simply delivering your child without the use of drugs and/or surgical procedures. You can have a natural childbirth at the hospital or at home, and there are a number of different approaches to natural childbirth that are available to people who choose this method.

Of course, you should be aware of the risks that come with any method of birthing, and have access to a trained physician if you choose this method, in case anything goes wrong. A lot of women choose the natural childbirth method and are very happy to endure the pain without painkillers, choosing alternative methods to deal with the birthing process.

Most of the methods can be described as combining relaxation techniques, breathing, mindfulness, and easing pain naturally. While each approach differs slightly, they all aim to ease the pain that comes with a drug-free birth. Some of the approaches that seem to be present in most techniques are:

Relaxation

Most methods will have a relaxation component that may include massage or finding different positions that ease the pain on back muscles or the belly muscles to ease the pain that develops there. Alternatives to laying on your back for delivery could include standing or squatting with support, allowing gravity to help with the birth, or giving birth in a bathtub or shower to alleviate the discomfort with the buoyancy of water.

Breathing

Breathing can also help alleviate the stress and pain with childbirth, by focusing the mind and having the woman concentrate on the breathing rather than the pain. This can help with focusing her energy on contractions, effectively "breathing through" them and not holding her breath or hyperventilating, both of which are not
good for her stress levels.

Mindfulness

There are many ways to focus the mind to take away the pain that is associated with childbirth. Some women will try hypnosis to focus their minds away from the pain, and onto the joys of having a baby. Others will find a talisman or a special amulet to hold on to when they are in contractions, to focus on and concentrate their energy into, in order to take their minds away from the pain. By concentrating on an object, they are able to be mindful of the moment, and minimize focusing on the pain.

CHAPTER 15
What Do You Need To Know About Parenting?

PARENTING IS NOT JUST

•A learning style.
•"how to" method to modify your child's behavior.
•Doing what your parents did.
•Doing what your parents didn't do.
•Getting it right every time.
•Copying experts that make money teaching you.

Parenting is the one job that you never retire from. Owner's manual not included should be the warning label placed on the child before and after birth. The baby needs and demands your help in every aspect. On the physical side: you feed, change the diaper, bathe, dress and put to sleep. On the psychological side: your smiles, mood and stress level help nurture the child's sense of safety and well being.

The obsession for our children to have more and be better than us undermines our love for them. We want the best for our children based on our subjective standard and the agenda of others. Often, we don't see our children as individuals and people with a heart and who willneed our love and guidance. Our love gives more than toys and the "best education". It is our love and time that is the "best gift to our children."

What can we do to guide and even influence our child? There are some factors parents can't influence and some they can. It is like the balance of a seed (nature) and soil (nurture). A seed sown and grown in good soil will grow. As parents, we can do our best to provide the best soil (environment) to nurture our children's development and growth. And that is all we can do. The nurture part is 50% which is our responsibility. The other 50% (nature) comes built in at birth with each child.

The 5 Learning Influences

•Play - All children learn through play. Play with them as they learn.
•Talk - Children speak the words you speak to them. More words heard, more words spoken.
•Listen - Use both ears and eyes to see and hear the sounds your child makes.
•Read - Children learn to read from seeing and hearing you read.
•Love - The secret ingredient of life and learning. Countless small acts and daily decisions comprise our lives.

Through the practice of 10 minute learning every day, we are laying a foundation of life-long learning.

How to Understand
What Good Parenting is About

Good parenting is important to all children and should help them become healthy in all parts of their lives. However, it will not necessarily prevent teenagers from doing the wrong things. Parenting is generally about balancing the support and control they receive from the right places and at the right times. Although we all have different personalities, as responsible parents we can all use our unique strengths to authoritatively guide our kids while also learning how to relate to them. You could also say it is all about the golden rule.

In many ways, it is simply about the positive attitude you show to your children. I have three children and I aim to do everything I can to ensure they will grow up to be happy and healthy. Children who grow up with "hands on" parents are half as likely to get into trouble as kids raised by "hands off" parents. But successful parenting is not about always being the bad guy just to keep your kids inline. It's also about making children want to be good on their own so you can enjoy watching them grow into responsible adults.

Raising good children is also a function of good marriage. The two are not separate. It's not a race to the finish line. It's more like a stroll.

The idea behind great parenting translates into being a support for the child.

Good parents should provide for their children's physical and emotional needs. It should be about providing a warm, secure home life that helps your child to learn the rules of life (e.g., you may have to stop them from doing things they shouldn't be doing, but it is just as important to encourage them to do the things you do want them to do).

Three Tips
for Parenting Success!

I believe there is no one way to parent. We are all different people with different family circumstances. In regards to good parenting, I think many of us agree that there are many roads that lead to Rome. So, I'm not going to try to tell you what you have to do or how you have to do it as a parent. I'm just going to give you three more tips to add to your arsenal of parenting strategies.

First, I want to point out that there is no such thing as quality time when it comes to effective parenting. Either you're there for your children or you're not. And I can certainly tell you that our kids want us to be there for them way more than they want us off saving the world somewhere else and only briefly popping into their lives in a whirlwind.

Another great tip to parenting is to build a strong food culture within your family. Countries like Italy and France that have strong food cultures also have strong family bonds. In other words, share a meal together and make it a family tradition. Now, I'm not saying to overindulge to the point where you all become unhealthy. I'm just saying that a family that breaks bread together tends to stay together.

Next, sometimes it's easier to parent other children than our own. We've all had one of our kid's friends over, and the friend was more polite and helpful than our own. This doesn't mean our kids are lacking something. It's just natural for our kids to put themselves on auto-pilot when they are around us and their friends, who don't really know us, to be on their best behaviors when around us.

CHAPTER 16
Positive Parenting!

Positive parenting! I like the ring to that, don't you? In a world, that is so tumultuous sometimes it really helps when our children can look to their parents as their positive role models. Parents, we can do this! It won't be easy, but we can do this. We can practice positive parenting and make a big difference in our children's lives. And someday they will then take our positive practices forward and make a positive difference in the lives of their children.

As positive parents who practice positive parenting, we all innately know that it is our parental duty to make sure that our kids feel protected and loved. We all have our own ways of doing this, so I'm not going to go into how to do it, okay? So, let's just make sure that all of our kids know they are protected and loved. The knowing is the tricky part. So, let's make sure that they know.

Next, as parents, it's imperative that mom and dad don't fight in front of the kids. I know this is easier said than done. But we must be vigilant about not looking combative in front of our children. Arguing in front of the kids scares our kids and makes them feel unsafe and torn between mom and dad. Let's air our marital disagreements in private, away from the eyes and ears of our children.

Also, let's set expectations and rules for our kids like bedtime, chores, and how they are supposed to treat others. When our kids don't live up to our expectations and rules, then let's discipline them out of love, rather than anger and resentment. Let's speak to them softly and help them understand the right and productive way to conduct themselves. We can have high expectations and be both firm and loving.

Positive
Parenting Plans

The Parenting Plan addresses any concerns the child may have like the need to maintain a relationship with both parents. It is very important that your children understand their relationship with both parents is forever and that they will never be abandoned. The Parent Coordinator can help explain that a divorce does not end your child's relationship with either parent. The marriage may end, however, the parent-child relationship will continue. Generally, for a child in a youth program or boarding school, short, clear explanations are best. Remember they do not have to understand everything all at once.

Their understanding of your divorce will evolve as they get older and will change with their age.

It is also a benefit that we will be able to work with their therapist in their behavior modification program or boarding school which means they will receive additional support. Another important message for kids to hear is that in no way is the divorce their fault, nor are they able to keep you together. When the idea of parents separating is completely new to your child, reinforce to them that you will make every effort to keep things stable for them. At the same time, let them know about upcoming changes. Remember children will ask the same questions repeatedly.

This is normal and is their way of gaining a sense of security and reassurance about the future. It is important to keep your answers simple and consistent.

It is very important that both parents reinforce that the separation/divorce is taking place because of differences between the parents. Working with your child's therapist in their program helps you conduct such conversations without damaging or disparaging remarks about the other parent. Children adjust more easily when parents show a healthy sense of respect and caring for the other parent despite difficult circumstances.

50

Co-parenting responsibilities apply to all parents whether they are married or divorced.

The extent that parents can effectively co-parent their children greatly determines how children will adjust after returning home from their emotional growth program or school. Parents who have a child returning home after graduation or completion of their program will now have to start dealing with more day-to-day issues concerning their child's welfare. Decisions, like those concerning religion, discipline, finances, morality, recreation, physical health, education and emergencies need to be discussed prior to their coming home.

These decisions need to be discussed and made jointly. Remember that married parents often have differing ideas about all or some of these issues. This is to be expected. There is no reason to assume that divorced parents should always agree on them either. What's important is how you deal with differences, not that they exist. It is better for parents to agree to disagree and practice compromising than to argue and fight endlessly for their own way. This however, is often easier said than done.

Parents who chose their battles and cooperate when there are differences are more likely to make healthy decisions for their children. In fact, nurturing an overall spirit of cooperation is more important than parents agreeing on any one particular issue. Also, parents who acknowledge and effectively deal with their own difficult feelings usually have an easier time. On the other hand, recurrent arguments between parents make life difficult for children and parents alike. When parents fight for their own agenda and neglect creating a peaceful environment, their children may develop bitter feelings and have difficulties later in life with their own intimate relationships.

Remembering to relate maturely and with a healthy sense of respect for the other parent (even in the face of great differences and in some cases bad feelings) is the challenge for every parent. Fostering such an environment teaches children much about love, life, change, and family relationships. Being in a family style program or outdoor school brings about many changes in the lives of both parents and children. One change for children may be in their immediate support network. This might mean a loss of friendships and school ties.

Some parents move to a new community before their child returns home.

This move might also include changing relationships with extended family members. To minimize stress on your children and ultimately yourself, work to keep your lifestyle close to what it was prior to your child being in their residential program or school.

When possible, keep friends, family, school, and other community support systems stable. When changes are necessary, make sure you give your children ample notice about them and discuss them with your child's therapist while still in their program. The more comfortable parents are with such changes the more comfortable their children will be. In the days just after your child returns home from their youth program, or wilderness program there is usually an adjustment period that can last for several weeks and oftentimes several months. During this time, people are adjusting to new routines, schedules, and living situations. It may take time for life to seem normal again.

Don't worry, eventually it will. Some kids are open about their feelings and the associated changes they experience. Others will be less vocal.

Make room for whatever your children are experiencing. It is a mistake to believe kids must talk about their feelings. Sample Checklist for a stable home environment after your child returns home from their program:

•Avoid too frequent changeovers between homes if this is a two household family.
•Be nurturing, supportive, and available.
•Create routines and schedules.
•Develop a firm parenting schedule that provides frequent and regular contact with the nonresident parent.
•Do not burden children with adult responsibilities.
•Do not rely on children to be your confidants or companions.
•End parental conflict, at least within the child's earshot.
•Provide clear rules and limits and be consistent
•Support children's relationships with their other parent and that parent's extended family.
•Seek out other sources of social support for your children.

A well-thought-out and executed parenting plan is an important tool for ensuring the health and well being of your children. A good parenting plan will outline how you will perform co-parenting responsibilities. It also details how you will handle activities of daily living and caring for your kids.

The parenting plan is a living document that must evolve with the needs of your growing children. Therefore, you do not have to include every potential situation you may encounter in the parenting plan. However, it must be revisited regularly to make sure it meets the needs of your family. Children are our most precious resource.

What Are Parenting Plan Issues?

Strict schedules at first in parenting plans are great for the children. Kids need the most stable environment parents can provide while in the middle of mediating conflict of resolution to many issues in their divorce. The parenting plan will be filed with the family court after the parents have worked the problems out among themselves. Strict schedules for child visitation will show the children both parents still love them and desire to stay connected to them.

Decide who pays for what. Think about compensation figures if expenses are higher at one household. School attendance may be a given for some children, but if not, it is important to decide who will determine where the kids will go to school. Some parents like to home school; others will want their kids in gifted or special education programs.

It should be determined who will go to parent-teacher conferences. It is important for your child to know that they are accountable to both parents for success in school. So, who will get the report cards and other notices?

Copies of these documents from school can be emailed as attachments very easily to the non-custodial parent. A website called foldershare.com is designed for kids to share these kinds of things with a parent who lives away.

After-school activities are another consideration when the kids get older. Document in your plan for child custody who will determine which after-school activities your child will be allowed to participate in.

Medical care is another topic to be included in documented parenting partnerships. Parents need to agree on paying for braces if needed and who will pay for medical care. The parent with medical benefits at work should be the one to provide medical and dental insurance coverage.

In the case of a medical emergency, decide who will make the ultimate decision for treatment. It is also important to consider when the non-custodial parent will be notified. In non-emergency medical situations like a cold or virus, who will decide if child visitation should be interrupted? Determine how parents will communicate with each other about medications the children may need to take from time to time.

Have you thought about elective surgery as a possibility for your child?
Of course, there are many other considerations to include in a parenting plan. These are the first thoughts for child custody during mediation in divorce. Transportation between households, access to the kids while they are away, planning for vacations and holidays, and child care are just some of the additional issues to be included in your parenting plan. Detail as much as you can to avoid problems for you and your children when the divorce is final.

All Things You Have to Know
About Parenting Techniques to Change the Bad Behavior of Your Children

If your children behave badly such as fighting, lying, stealing, lazy to do some homework, denial, or interrupting when the parents are on the phone you would feel disappointed. That attitude which the child has was perfectly natural course.

But do not allow it to persist, you should take appropriate action. The problem is what are the appropriate actions that we should take? Here I will show you some techniques you have to know about parenting to change the bad behavior of your children.

In order to cope with the bad behavior is not easy. It needs more attention and seriousness from the parents. The first thing you can try is to give clear instructions and give the child a reason why you told himlike that. For example when you prohibit them from jumping on the bed. Just try to give an explanation that if they jump on the bed it can cause damage and so on. That way; children will understand why you are prohibiting them.

Of course, your positive attitude means a lot in the process of educating children. So that respecting the child and providing support when a child needs your help are a must to be practiced. With such attitudes, the parents would see the child as a human being, who is learning, not as an obstacle.

When your child has been playing too long and it is time to sleep, try to remind himfive or ten minutes earlier. That way, your child knows that he has to stop playing. So that when the time actually comes, he will not argue with you because he has prepared himself to stop playing.